THE BUTCHERKNIFE
AND
THE MOCKINGBIRD

A Poetry Collection

by Holly Wright

Holly Wright

The Butcherknife and the Mockingbird

Cover design by Holly Wright
Author photo by Joe Helsel

Printed in the United States of America
ISBN: 9798573072838

Content Warning:

Suicide, Self-Harm, Depression, Anxiety

Holly Wright

The Butcherknife and the Mockingbird

author's note
This collection is about both romance and
heartbreak, and mental health and healing.
While the two topics are mixed together, it's
important for readers to understand that the two
are not related to each other. Love cannot heal
someone depressed. Depression is not (always)
caused by heartbreak. This is simply my story—
two journeys through two things that have
shaped who I am as a person.

Holly Wright

The Butcherknife and the Mockingbird

*With immeasurable thanks to Nick, Joe, my
mother, and my sister*

"The Butcherknife"

How much would it hurt
to hack my heart to pieces

Can I break it more than it's already been broken?
Can I carve the pieces so fine
you can't see them?

(if you can't see it you can't hurt it
please, god,
don't hurt me
anymore)

Maybe I'll bleed to death
finally
instead of continue in this half-existence

Locked in my head
locked in my suffering
lost in my breaking

It can't hurt half as much
as I already do

This knife
will surely hurt less

than this life

Holly Wright

"August 27, 2013"

7 years ago today
I met the boy who would break my heart

I was fifteen
with a blistered soul and breaking
heart
I walked around like I was dying
to crawl out of my own skin

I met a boy
too tall for his comfort, always slouching
but who spoke like he was commanding
the sky
with sparkling eyes and a soul shattering smile

I walked in the room
met his eyes
and the universe shifted into place—
a fractured bone healing

Our introduction made the heavens tremble with want
Our knotted lifelines made planets collapse
Because he saw me
saw *me* and not just who I pretended to be

I was lost at sea
and his eyes were lighthouses beckoning me to safety

I always felt safe with him

But I never said what I should have

3

The Butcherknife and the Mockingbird

The lighthouse burned out
the keeper abandoned the ship to the sea
and all I had left was an echo of a smile
that scathed my soul

We ended the way we began
Strangers
staring in awe

I am haunted by the words
I should have said

All I know of love
is tangled up in heartbreak

"Infatuation"

I've loved rarely
felt that swell of need, want, passion, and pain
four times
So rarely
but it's devoured me

My bones splintered beneath my skin
because they rotted with want
My heart bled through my fingertips
because it melted beneath the heat of my passion

And my soul
my soul was stolen from me
and left me aching and hollow and desperate

I want to be loved so badly
I would carve my heart out
of my chest to give it to you

(I know it's bloody, but doesn't it make a lovely red
ribbon?)

I'll give you everything

My courage,
my will,
my heart,
my soul,
my

everything

The Butcherknife and the Mockingbird

I'll dress it up however you want
What package looks prettiest?

It's consuming me
this need
this impossible need

Do you want the stars?
I'll rip them from the sky
inject them into your veins, bury them in your bones

Or maybe you want the sea
drained and empty and gone forever
I'll drink 'til the salt scalds my throat raw
for you I swear I will

For you I'll light the world on fire
and paint your likeness in the ashes

What do you want?
Tell me what you want, and I'll do it
if it means I own your heart

What do you want?

I'll carve my own bones into a treasure chest
to keep it safe;
just let your heart be mine

"Ode to Loneliness"

Imagine
singing (screaming)
at a pitch no one
else could hear
Imagine
existing wholly and completely alone
in a universe with billions
of other life forms

Sometimes I'm scared to breathe out
because I wonder if
this time
my breath will be a scream
I'm scared if I scream
no one's going to hear me

People ask me
often
about the tattoo on the back of my neck
What I tell them is
"I like whales"
when what I mean is

I cried for an hour the first time
I ever heard about The Loneliest Whale in the World

I wanted to find the deepest spot in the ocean
point to the bottom
swallow my fear
say "there"
and dive

The Butcherknife and the Mockingbird

because the loneliest girl
should befriend the loneliest whale

(I know he can hear me)
(I am convinced I will hear him)

I wanted the waves
hissing along the shore
to instead
echo with my grief

because if a tree falls and no one
is there to hear it,
does it make a sound
If a foghorn calls out in the dark
and nothing answers back
is it really standing there

And if I cry out my pain
on a crowded planet
and no one turns to find me
am I actually here

None of the other whales can hear him
Ray Bradbury wrote "The Foghorn"
in 1951
39 years before the 52-hertz whale was ever heard
A sea monster wailed back to the foghorn
convinced it was alone in the world
and destroyed the one thing that made it believe
that maybe it wasn't alone after all

I have to tell him he's not alone

Maybe Ray Bradbury knew
Maybe the lonely people always know

I am the girl
standing at the edge of the ship
like I am always on the edge
with my back to the lighthouse
that's still calling me back to safety

and I'm screaming at the captain
"dive!"
and he's yelling back
"this isn't a submarine!'

And I'm laughing
And I'm crying
And I'm begging

"Do it anyway"

because I need to find him
because I need someone to find me
I am the girl
always on the edge
Always willing to dive

And sometimes I am the whale
Sometimes I am the sea monster

I am always the foghorn,
desperate to be heard,

endlessly singing
back to myself

Holly Wright

"Haunted"

I see your face in crowds when you're not there
I practice saying your name
because the weight of it could tilt the earth
and I want to get it right
It's the most beautiful word I know

Your smile burns through my dreams
Your voice is a thunderclap
drowning out everything else
I hear you saying my name
over and over and over
A prayer to dead gods
that's never going to be answered

Or maybe it's the other way around
and all my dreams are wishes
made on burned out candles and burned out stars

Never coming true

It'd be easier if you were dead
Maybe then I could let you go
I wouldn't look for you in every crowded room
I wouldn't think your voice is the one I hear calling my
name
and I wouldn't be devastated every time
I turn around and see you're gone

It'd be easier if you were a ghost
because then I'd have proof you were here

11

But all I have are taunting whispers
and faded memories
and a burning hope

maybe you'll come back

and be more than just the thing that haunts me

"Duality"

My life has always been half
looking down the barrel
of the gun and waiting for the spark

and half staring through the eye
of the noose
waiting for a reason

My heart wants shelter
in the stained glass quiet
is willing to drop to its knees and beg
forgiveness

My feet are already fleeing
the hallowed marble halls and scorching
the earth where I touch it

Because I try so hard to be good
but I'm still a sinner
and I don't know if I'll ever make it out
in time

My life has always been me
ready to fling myself off a cliff
just to prove I can
and run
across the country on a dare
just because someone told me
"Never stop running"

The Butcherknife and the Mockingbird

But my feet won't move
I never jump; I always fall
and the running is only ever so far
that it makes me want to look back
and see what I'm missing

My shipwrecked soul
is certain I should go
My heart is a broken lighthouse
begging me to stay

My hands are ice
but my heart is warm, I promise

I can't help who I am
I can't help who I want to be

I have always been in pieces

(I'm waiting
to be put back together)

Holly Wright

"Identity"

To them,
I'm the weird girl

I'm the girl with her earbuds jammed in her ears,
tapping her foot in time with a beat no one else can hear
while she scrawls words no one else will read

screaming on blank white pages
because if she screams out loud she's a freak

That's who I am to them

But I've killed myself a hundred times
today
I don't even know who else I can be
and I promise
you can't loathe me,
mock me,
torment me more
than I do myself

my fury and my pain
are sharks in the water
circling ever closer
endlessly

My joy is a flickering match
about to burn out
and burn my life down with it
I am constantly on the brink
of every exhale becoming ash

The Butcherknife and the Mockingbird

This page is saving my life
This beat is stepping in for my vacant heart

I'm a weird girl
it's true

But what else can I be
without wanting to die?

Holly Wright

"A Canary Singing"

I don't think I have organs
I think I have bombs

There's something inside me
waiting to explode
A dam is cracking
spilling
bursting

There are mines buried in my lungs,
rats crawl over my skin and claw off my flesh
the air is souring and poisonous,
and the silence is deafening

I am terrified of the ceaseless way my mind tears
itself apart

and this hollow countdown
to my eruption

I am petrified
dying a slow and painful death inside my skin
terrified of the way my mind works
and my body heeds it

I am in constant terror
I can hardly breathe

Can you hear the canary's song?

All I hear is ticking

"Consumed"

Devour me

I wanted that kind of love.
The kind that makes you shake,
the kind that terrifies you.

The one that makes you stare
sightless
at the ceiling in the middle of the night
because you can't sleep.
You can never sleep.

You can barely breathe.

Ravish me

I dreamt
of a love so sweet
it rotted my bones.
The reality was more painful.

It was an all-consuming kind of love.
It coiled around my spine,
swallowed my heart,
latched onto my throat.

It was less like an embrace
and more like a stranglehold.
Not the touch of a lover,
but the strange and terrible grip of a killer.

Holly Wright

Let me go

I wanted to love you.
It was all I wanted.

I wanted the pain. I invited
it in. But you—
you had sharper teeth than I thought

What should have been love bites
drained me
Left black bruises across my soul

I don't want this love
anymore
I want to be able to breathe

"Astral"

I'm a wraith, floating through my life.
I look in mirrors and can't believe what I'm seeing.
I haunt my own skin.

My thoughts are real,
I think,
but if I have to wonder
are they really?

Maybe I'm made up.
Maybe I'm the most elaborate dream I've ever had.
I only exist to me.

I'm a ghost
pretending to be alive.

I only exist if someone sees me.

"Do you ever doubt the existence of others around you?"
"No,
I usually doubt my own."

(can anyone see me?)

Holly Wright

"Cupid and Psyche"

Scars riddle my skin where your lips burned
against me

Your promise to love me
me
as I am

Not loathe me as a monster, a thief
who stole your most precious belonging

(your beating heart,
ripped from the bars of your ribcage
clenched in my fist)

nor worship me as a god
too exquisite to simply love

(your adoration
would be a noose tangled
around your love like my hands in your hair)

Your promise to love me
me
as I am

tore my flesh apart
and laid me bare,
exposed, raw, aching, dying over and over and

over again

I was never
worth your love

You sought me in places
I could never reach
You loved me in ways

that broke me
And I would give anything
anything

to have never loved you

Your ghost will haunt me through eternity
and I will love you
I will love you
I will always love you
(in the dark,
in the candlelight,
in secret)

against my will

"Masquerade"

When we're born,
we're born brand new
with shiny, smiling faces,
few flaws, and perfect
innocence.
Our minds are not yet
cracked and uncertain,
claimed and contaminated
by thoughts not our own.
We are whole,
happy,
open.

Then, something changes.
The fat in our faces
gives way to smoother, sharper
planes with a host of blemishes.
Our minds
are plagued with doubt,
worry--
insecurities implanted by people we seek approval from.
We begin to hide who we really are
to please everyone else.
We humans classify this as
"growing up."

It happens again,
this process,
except now our faces
are weathered grooves
of pain, loss,

and never being good enough.
These are scars,
etched in our skin and
more permanent than tattoos
on our minds,
which are no longer innocent,
fresh, or our own,
They're tinged with society's
lies and expectations,
which we all fail to meet.

There is darkness in our heads,
very little light in our eyes.
Just remember this
when you die.

We've all hidden ourselves away
behind masks that we all hate,

And by the time you want to take it off
it's much, much too late.

This is my life, and yours.
Welcome to the dance.

Holly Wright

"Holding On"

I dreamt of him again last night
The boy with the black hair and brown eyes
darling eyes
The shape of his smile is still imprinted on my skin

You're supposed to let people go
I know
Cut the strings of the kite and let it fly
away, let the balloon go with your wishes still attached

You're not supposed to hold on so tightly
your palms are bleeding

I know
I know

But how do you let go of the person
who taught you the worth you hold,
who made you think the earth was a better place
with you in it,
and the words you had to say
mattered, and the fears you harbored
didn't have to be so scary

Even in the dark
Especially in the dark

The Butcherknife and the Mockingbird

There are people who break walls down
with the tips of their fingers
and the curve of their lips
like their entire body is poised for destruction
with the strength of their kindness

Their love is a wrecking ball

He was a wrecking ball to my life
I have never been the same

Because I was the loneliest girl in the world
and he was the only person who heard me
screaming

How am I supposed to let that go?

I don't believe in soulmates
I don't

But maybe some souls are carved from the same
stars, their origins bind them to each other,
their love is tangled in their creation

I loved him
I can still feel my lifelines knotted with his

I'm happy now
In love
Living a life I only dreamed of

Without him

But after all this time
I still always
think of the boy with black hair
and darling eyes
who taught me the secrets of hearts
and all the love they can hold

And I wonder if his palms are bleeding, too

"Empty"

it's not your fault they broke me
it's not your fault you're not him
but when i opened my legs for you i need to know
you knew you weren't going to reach my heart
i don't think i have one
my chest is hollow
my soul is stolen
i have nothing left to give
except my body
you can have that
but it's all you can have
i won't love you
i promise i won't
i'm too afraid
to ever love again

believe me
when i say my chest is empty

"First Time"

I am fascinated by people
and the way they live
and breathe
so effortlessly.

I like to watch them dance—
twirling
dipping
sinking inside the beats of drums,
ignoring the beats of the hearts
they carry themselves.

I don't dance.
I don't know how.
I have absolutely no
sense of rhythm,
I cannot carry a tune to save my life.
My legs can barely carry my body.

I sometimes wonder,
watching everyone else,
if my inability
is the lack of something else.

Because I see them,
all of them,
all the flush in their cheeks
and breath puffing out of their lungs
and the pulse in their necks—
but I don't think a single one of them
sees me.

The Butcherknife and the Mockingbird

And I think I can't keep a beat,
because I don't have a heart that does.

I think I might be invisible.
I think I might be dying
or already dead.
I feel like I might be actively
ceasing to exist;
I can feel myself fading
and being forgotten
and it hurts a lot more than I ever imagined
it would.

I felt like I didn't exist
and that was the first night
I slit open my skin
just to see the blood
pump out
in time with the heartbeat
I wasn't sure was there.

Just to prove to myself I was
alive.

To prove I could still feel.

"One Night Stands"

Do you know the kind of hollow
it takes being
to need another person to fill you up?

The "never-let-me-go"
kind of desperate
it takes to cling for dear life
to whoever happens to be closest?

I do.

I know emptiness that feels like I am full of holes
(bullet wounds)
and all my insides
(all my hope)
are falling out.

I know that the way someone looks at me makes me feel
terrified
and exhilarated
(but fuck at least I feel something.)

I remember the way he looked at me.

I wanted it to hurt him.
I wanted him to want me so much it hurt
to look at me.

But the last boy I wrapped my legs around
just called me hot—
I thought

The Butcherknife and the Mockingbird

"Jesus, I hope so
since I'm already naked beneath you."

And the boy before that was unnervingly
gentle.
"Are you okay?"
(would you tell me if you weren't?)
Another gave me the best sex of my life
and a fat lip.
(It was an accident,
truly, he didn't know how easy I was to throw)
My favorite asked me to wake him
if I had my nightmares
(I want you to feel safe here.)
The first…
I wish the first had loved me.
(I wish I had loved him.)

I only knew one's first name,
and the fact that he didn't want to meet my eyes.
I can't watch Zootopia because
one of them couldn't wait anymore.

I would've given anything for the one who stayed
to leave
but I couldn't convince my mouth to do anything but kiss
him.
And one,
a friend,
told me I helped him get over his ex.

All of them looked at me.
But all that existed in their eyes

was hunger.

I've seen animals gaze more kindly
at their prey.

I wanted to change my mind,
to quiet the animal inside of me that said,
"Do it."
And the even quieter voice that said,
"Let him do it."

I thought, every time,
"This will be different."

And I never knew what a good liar I was
until I convinced myself it was true.

And every time,
I did feel something besides that resounding emptiness.

(People who leap from buildings fall so fast
because emptiness weighs so much.)

Maybe jumping from the roof of a skyscraper
or a bridge
or a mountain
would have been easier.

The Butcherknife and the Mockingbird

(I just wanted to feel alive,
feel loved,
feel saved.)

Maybe if I had done that
instead of letting them touch me
(they pushed me over the edge)
I wouldn't have been dying inside
after every kiss.

I wouldn't have hated my reflection in the mirror,
or felt so dirty I didn't think I would ever be clean again.
Maybe
I wouldn't have cried like I was trying to drown myself.

Maybe it would've been better
to stay hollow.

"7 deadly sins"

"Greed"

I want

I want to feel electric
60% of me shocking the world

Scorching the ground where I walk
I want passion

Furious, hungry, all-consuming
passion to swallow me whole

In an insipid world
overwhelmed by the mundane

I want

*

"Lust"

Every smile was an invitation
every laugh a plea

"Take me home
I can't be alone tonight"

I was water
and his body against mine an oil slick

But I didn't care
At least he was next to me

And my halved heart
was whole for a night

I wonder what his name was

*

"Wrath"

Forgiving isn't my job
I don't care about peace

I want justice
I want pain felt by those who cause it
I want their spines crushed

Their bones to turn to dust
beneath my heel

Regret won't be just a word

It will be an experience
And forgiveness will hang by its neck in the yard

alongside their bodies
swaying in the wind

*

"Envy"

I have everything
some people dream of

But there's more in the world
Other people have more

love, money, fame,
happiness

And I want it for myself so badly
my desire smolders in my heart

I am choking on desire
strangling on my own jealousy
burning inside my skin
dying to crawl out of it
and into someone else's life

I want what they have
what I don't
what I can't

I have everything
and it is not enough

*

"Gluttony"

On the nights when the pain is drowning me
(every night)

The Butcherknife and the Mockingbird

I'd rather drown in a bottle

I love the way it leaves me numb
I love the way the lights spin the way my mind does
(out of control)

I love the way I forget my own name
and yours

The warmth like poison in my blood
better than the razor blades that used to spill it

I get another drink to get happier
I get another drink and it's never enough

and one too many

*

"Sloth"

You think I don't want to do it
I do

But I can't
My limbs are stone

My brain is a statue frozen
infecting my lungs
my heart
my spine

I want to move

but I can't
I can barely breathe

I know you don't see it
But I can't do anything

*

"Pride"

I can do this on my own

You can't force me to admit I can't
You would have to drag the words from my decaying lungs
my severed tongue
before I'd ever say them willingly

 I would rather dig my own shallow grave
and bury myself alive
than admit I need you

I don't
I can do this on my own

Even when I can't

*

"A Heart, A Graveyard"

I told my best friend
we don't have a choice in who
we love.
Not really.
People tear us open,
rip apart the bars of the cages
that are our ribs,
dig their graves,
smile,
and bury themselves.
In our chests,
our cores.
In the hollowed out spaces of our hearts
they want to call home.

I can still taste dirt on my tongue
from the first boy I fell
for.
Still cough over the name
of the second
because his ashes
strangle my lungs.

My best friend told me
he thought it was strange
how we can remember
emotions
without really feeling them.

Holly Wright

Like we're haunted by our own love.
Carrying the ghosts
of living people
inside our chests,
prisoners in cages of flesh and bone and desire.

I wonder how many people
stumble over my name,
who feel heavier because of the weight
of me in their hearts.
If any do at all.
Or if the only person haunted,
the only person constantly
terrified
by the depth of their own love,
is me.

I wonder if he will ever be
just a name
to me.
A soft reminder I carry
in the depths of my being
that I'm not as untouchable as I like
to pretend.
Or if he will always,
always
make me wonder what it takes
to stop feeling
like I'm digging my own grave
or tearing myself in half
whenever he looks at me.

I think I will always be haunted
and I think
the only ghosts I carry
are the ones I created.

"Hourglass"

Eventually
I imagine there will be a day
when I don't wonder
at the nature of heartbeats

I won't stop
frozen
terrified
by the sound of my own

It won't be foreign
My pulse beneath my skin
will be something revered
awed
and not a waiting canvas
Not a zipper for my pain

I imagine
someday
I won't look at a bridge
and wonder how long the fall would take
If I would be able to count the seconds
like seconds on a bomb
If it would hurt when I landed
Like it has always hurt when I landed

Someday
my mind won't constantly
be tearing itself apart inside my skull

The Butcherknife and the Mockingbird

The battle will bow
to peace
and the thundering in my ears
and rib cage
will cease to sound like fleeing
victims
and instead sound like
a sigh of relief

I hope
one day
I'll finally be able to breathe
without wanting to scream

I hope
one day
I'll own my life
instead of letting my fear

Holly Wright

"A Sidewalk Conversation"

I've always imagined street lamps
as miniature
man-made moons

The streetlight and the stars
were the only ways I could see
your face
and I couldn't see your eyes

But that's because you weren't looking at me
You were somewhere far away
Maybe the future
because that's what we were talking about

(I don't remember why
I don't remember what we said
I remember you were sad
and I couldn't stop thinking
of all the ways I wanted to make you happier)

Or maybe the past
(because that's the only place we
really exist together
now)

I blinked
and we were fifteen years old
and I wasn't staring at your face in the moonlight
I was looking at your name in the light of my phone
and your words
because I always fell asleep before you

45

The Butcherknife and the Mockingbird

"Just in case,
I love you."

Your words buried themselves in my bones
Masqueraded for years as my beating heart
(I am a graveyard of you)

I blinked
and then we were fourteen
and my dress was the night sky
stars sprinkled in satin
and your eyes were brighter than the moon
And your tentative hands on my waist and awkward
laugh
were tourniquets around every wound that ever split me
open

I blinked again
We were both eighteen
I was laughing up at you
and you were calling me the light
that cuts through the never ending darkness
and drudgery of every day life
while our friends giggled
and called us the platonic power couple
Then I was in your arms
and you were smiling as wide as me
(a light cutting through the dark)
and the world was rebuilding itself
to fit the way your arms molded around me
like home
while the camera rolled on
immortalizing a moment I'd already

Holly Wright

captured
and memorized
so that when I would forget to breathe
at least I remembered you

I didn't want to blink again
afraid to miss a moment with you
(all my favorite moments
are made up of you)
I didn't want to relive those memories
I was afraid
I'd wear them too thin
they'd become too-handled photographs
faded

And I wish we hadn't talked about the future
because I didn't know
you weren't going to be a part of mine

I would've told you
how scared I was of losing you
I would've told you that every time you smiled at me
my heart broke

(I would've tried to give you
as much of me
as you gave me of you

I know it doesn't sound like much
but every time I inhale it feels like you
and my exhales sound like your name)

The Butcherknife and the Mockingbird

I remember you looked at me
eyes dancing as brightly
as my man-made moons

and infinitely more beautiful

And I wish I would've captured
that moment
because I didn't know it would be the last
one I had a chance to

Holly Wright

"Je T'aime"

 I don't speak French
You do
so all I know how to say is "hello"
"goodbye"
and "I love you"

(I know
I could love you forever
I will love you forever
And you still would never stay
You are always walking
away)

And "I miss you"

Tu me manques.

I am walking around with a hole in my chest
because I don't
just
miss you
You are missing from me
Essential to my existence
(you are
the beat that is always skipped
in my heart rhythm)

I smile
and I always look to see if you're smiling
too because I look for you in every room
you're the only face I ever look for

The Butcherknife and the Mockingbird

You are the only person I want
to tell everything to
in any language
you want to hear it in
I'd learn French for you and I hate
French

You are my favorite person to exist

(please break my ribs like the bars of a cage
build your home in my heart
because you're my home)

I think the gap between my ribs
where my heart stutters
is shaped like your smile
on the day when I told you that you
and I were going to get married

and then kill each other
because you don't like one of my favorite
bands

Yes
I meant that
We'll make headlines baby
because the second we said hello
was a second that's been five hundred years coming

(and the moment we're going to say goodbye
has been coming just as long)

We used to talk
every night
(in English
thank god)
about everything
I know everything about you
everything you never told another soul
We usually fell asleep
before dawn broke
but we never missed a step
never missed a breath the next morning
We were always
on the same page
sharing the same thought
dancing to the same beat

(but at 3 am
the only ones alive
are the lovers
and the unloved
the broken
the damned
and the lost
At 3 am
I used to tell you
I loved you
and I missed you
and you echoed those words back
and we never said
goodbye

The Butcherknife and the Mockingbird

And now at 3 am
I stare with burning eyes
at the ceiling and talk to empty space
thinking of you
and you're sleeping next to her
and my love is shredded
in ribbons
I am heartbroken
holding my bleeding heart in my hands)

Hello
I miss you
Goodbye

And I don't know if you'll ever read this
but

just in case,

Je t'aime

Holly Wright

"Mourning Birds"

Why do we assume birds are singing?

Maybe we've mistaken their agony for beauty.

Maybe those lovely notes are cries of pain.

All their screams mistaken for songs,
anguish mistaken for joy.

And all the birds are mourning birds.
And all the birds are weeping.

And none of us know the difference.

"My Favorite Part"

There's a moment between the falling and the landing
when nothing hurts
when I'm fearless
when I think you're going to catch me

You were my best friend
I thought you would always be my safe place to land

That moment was my favorite part
because it was the moment before you walked away

Before the pain

I've broken over two dozen bones in my body
My skeleton has broken more
than you'd think a heart would

But every break combined
hurt less than this

You love her
and not me

That's not true
You love me
I know you love me
But you love me less

You love me so much less than I love you
I didn't think you did

Holly Wright

(I really thought you would catch me)

I miss that moment
The freedom in the falling
The fearlessness in the hope

~~I miss you~~
I can't say that anymore

I wish I could go back
Rewind
Pause

And live in that part
for just a little longer

"Alone"

I feel fragmented
all my edges blurred
and splintering
in a million directions
I try to pull myself together but the shards
slit my palms and I always lose
my grip
I can never find my way back to myself
I think I will always be broken

Holly Wright

"Flatline"

My smile is the saddest smile I've ever seen
It's a flat line
a dead heartbeat

I have a smile like a ghost
like it was there, it had a soul, and now it's just an echo lost
in time
a time stamp of when there was real joy,
frozen and lifeless and there
somehow

I don't think people see joy
when they look at me

I know they don't
They see sadness
crushing grief

I'm sorry all you can see is darkness
I'm sorry it bleeds
from me like I opened my veins
I know there used to be light somewhere
inside, but the darkness is all
I have left
it's the only gift I can give

Maybe someday I can be the girl the world
and god
and my family loved

The Butcherknife and the Mockingbird

I'm sorry she's gone
now

I'm sorry this smile
is all I have

Holly Wright

"Moving On"

I could tell you about the long nights
when he taught me how to laugh
how to feel
how to breathe

how to love

When the only thing I knew better than him
was the way the stars rise
and twinkle like they're never going to burn
out

like a pinky promise made in the dark
to only ever be a wish
and not a black hole

I could tell you about the songs
that froze time
When dancing was the most beautiful
painful
awkward thing

I think we looked like penguins
always wobbly

I could tell you about the days
my heart split at the seams in its cage
because he was going to leave me
He was always going to leave me

The Butcherknife and the Mockingbird

I was always going to leave him
And the months after
when we drifted back into each other's orbits
gravity defied by our pull together

All those moments blur together

(curioushappyinloveconfusedcrushedlosthopeful)

He is scored on my heart
I will always remember us this way

Laughing
Dancing
Telling secrets in the dark
Standing hopelessly in a stairwell
(never saying the words I wanted to say most)
Watching each other walk away

I could tell you all about the long nights
and beautiful days
and agonizing
wonderful
memories

Instead I'll tell you only this

We both deserved better

Holly Wright

"War Zone"

In my mind
it's a war zone

I'm a single person caught in a maelstrom
of whistling bullets and exploding grenades
Debris and shrapnel are tearing me apart
shredding me to bits

In my mind
I'm screaming
and no one can hear me above the *boom* of the world
self-destructing

I am trapped here
in a loop
every day

Some days the bullets change to arrows
and the death is all that much slower
The tips sink into my flesh, protruding from my back
my ribs
my skull

I am full of wounds and I am falling

I keep waiting for the day that the war stops
when someone waves a white flag
or calls a truce
or wins

but I think this war is waiting for me to die

The Butcherknife and the Mockingbird

I never stood a chance
I should've grabbed a gun and ended it myself
wrapped a pair of dog tags around my neck and said,
"Don't worry, boys,
they're not mine"

I hold my breath sometimes
anyway
like if I do they won't see me
the bullets will miss my body

But the agony rips through me anyway
Every day
Every day every past trauma rears up
and tries to kill me

My will to live
my ability to stand and face the day
is tested
and I want to quit
I want to fail
I want to let go

The holding on is so painful
The holding on is just killing me slower

Holly Wright

"The Party"

I know I shouldn't do this
I know it'll pull me under
but the lights are low
and the smiles are encouraging
me to do it anyway, to take a drink
and a second one
and a third
and

and I can't breathe

the room is spinning
or I am
out of control

Small spaces and smaller hearts,
shallow breaths and shallow cuts

And red
So much red

I can trace the map of my wreckage through broken bottles
broken hearts
and spread legs

I know the destruction I'm drowning in
originated at the bottom of a bottle
and a boy's bed
and his blue eyes

The Butcherknife and the Mockingbird

when I couldn't breathe
or think

and now I can barely function

This bed will be my death bed
The silence in this dorm room will be my eulogy

I'm going to die here

or maybe I already did
and this is just where they'll find my body

Holly Wright

"The night I decided to kill myself"

I wasn't sure I was real
it didn't feel like killing
me, you see, I was killing someone else
someone who lived in the mirror
and my skin
and my skeleton
I was so far away from the person I knew
I used to be, my death
was happening to someone else
I was so numb
inside my own body
I didn't think I'd even feel it

It didn't hurt by the way
It felt like peace
It felt like a room with all the windows open
a million ways of escape and all the fresh air
and I could breathe
for the first time in years

I wasn't sure I was real
And I wasn't sure someone unreal could be loved

But I loved
with whatever ruins passed for a heart in my chest
I loved

So I closed the windows
I felt myself suffocating

And I picked up the phone

65

"Letting Go"

In all this world
the one thing I wanted most
was you.

I wanted your heartbeat,
thundering under my touch.

I wanted your smile,
designed just for me,
blooming the moment I walked in the room.

I wanted many things,
all of them to do with you.

But you—
you never wanted me.

If you did, it was too late.
We were miles and years and ages apart.
We were different people than the ones who met
and maybe loved each other.

And maybe I did.
Maybe I did love you.
Maybe you loved me.

But now the thing I want
is no longer you.
I want it to not be you.
I want to let you go.

Please,
let me let you go.

"Suicide/Love Notes"

When I told you how much I loved
you, I meant it

I know I sent that text at two in the morning
when even the birds
were silent
sleeping
peaceful

I was peaceful, too

But I had to know you knew
my heart was so full it was going to break
with all my love for you

I had to know you knew
before I wasn't there to tell you
anymore

You made my time
here so wonderful
You took so much of my pain away

But I was so full of it
it drowned out everything
else... even my love

I didn't want to leave you
Not ever
and not like this

But I want you to know
when I tried to
I knew I would miss you most

I never meant to leave a suicide note
I didn't need to detail the reasons
I wanted to die

No
I needed to tell you
you were a reason to stay

This was my love note
for you
So you never had to doubt
if you were the reason why

I promise
I loved you
You were the reason why not

"The Healing"

He asked me if I ever wondered if anyone else was real

And I told him the truth
I wonder if I am

He thought that was fascinating
like I'd given him the cure to cancer
or the secret to the universe
or a reason to live

But the truth is, he gave me a reason

He was never scared
He never shied away from all my edges
sharp, jagged, deadly
he maneuvered around them
like they were just the thorns on a rose

Still worth having

I tried to walk away
I tried so hard

But he wouldn't let me go
He asked me if I really wanted to

And I didn't

I was scared
So scared
Trembling in my skin

Holly Wright

Breathing air that didn't reach my lungs

My shattered heart pounding so hard
I thought it was a countdown to a bomb

But my broken heart was proof
I had one

And I thought it belonged to him

"Winter"

Someone told me once
I remind them of winter

Beautiful
but cold
harsh
dark

Breathing me in
froze their lungs
My skin made their fingertips ache

But you
you love winter

How gently the snow falls
like the flakes have nothing better to do
than drift down to kiss the earth
And the way the darkness can't
grip the world,
not really,
because the clouds hang low and heavy
and drench us in a half-light

And everything is magic

I never thought about how soft
cold could be
How easily ice melts
turns to water

folds to whoever is warm enough
to make it want to thaw

You make me want to thaw

"Isn't Death Easier?"

Jumping from a building might have been easier
than telling my mom I wanted to die

I could have slit my throat
and it would have been less painful than forcing the words
(help me)
off my tongue

Drifting off to sleep
would have been better than feeling his pitying eyes on my
skin

Feeling my lungs fill with water
probably would have hurt
Not as much as hearing my best friend file a report about
how he was worried about me
like worrying was enough to stop me from dying while I still
had a heartbeat

I wish I was braver
I would have ended it and put us all out of our misery

The shame wouldn't engulf me like flames
The panic wouldn't swallow my mom like a black hole
The doctor would have room for someone else

But that's a lie

Maybe it would be less painful
maybe it would be less shameful
for me

but I would destroy the people I left behind

Death wraps his arms around whole families
not individuals
Death's fingers toy with the hearts of the living
when someone they love dies

My heartbeat isn't mine
My heartbeat belongs to them

Dying might have been preferable
But for them,
I'll fight for my life

"K.A.M."

I'm choking on my fear
and it tastes like every smile
you've given me
It tastes like your name
on the tip of my tongue
like someone
on the edge of a cliff
preparing to throw themselves
off the side
Preparing to die

My skin
doesn't stretch enough to
cover my bones
every time we talk
I'm overexposed
naked in a way clothing doesn't fix
and I don't even want my
clothes on
not with you
But I can't breathe
Your eyes punched a hole
in my lungs
and I wasn't ready
I'm still not ready

A heartbeat is a stupid thing
Fragile
timid
destroyed by very word
you say to me

Holly Wright

I have no rhythm
I have no way of holding on
to myself, my sanity, my courage
because you send terror flooding through me
with a single word

I thought
for a second
that I couldn't do this
I could not cut myself open
and let someone else in
because that's never been in the cards
never been a possibility in my brain

I had one foot out the door
and then I thought about the way
you said
my name
Two syllables have never
stopped me
in my tracks
never dragged my breath from my body
or steadied my erratic
desperate
always in-flight heart
Or made me want to stay

I want to stay
Just for a minute
I want to see if I can grow
see if I can breathe

"Burn"

I took my memories
lined them up one by one
smiled
and

set them on fire
shot them down
buried them each alive

and relished in their screams
I took the chains they bound me in
and wrapped them back
around their neck
turned my torture into their noose

fires only burn where there's oxygen
are only kept alive if they're fed

I'm stealing all the air
keeping it for myself
my life is the only one still burning
the rest of my pain will only be smoke

I won't let my memories
suffocate me
scorch my lungs and my skin
and leave me raw
aching
begging to die

Holly Wright

I'll own them
keep them in an urn in my heart
but they'll never hurt me again

I'm going to burn
I'm going to love it

"Falling"

I think I'm going to fall
I think I'm going to break
no,
I'm going to shatter
and I'm going to welcome
the pain
because
your moans sound like my new
favorite song
and the way your heart beats
settles the world,
your pulse ends wars
your smile strips me bare
strips me to the bone
leaves me naked and vulnerable
and I know you'd never break me
not on purpose
your naked
flesh is tearing me apart
tearing me wide open and forcing me
to lay my heart down before you
your skin under my skin
is destroying me
but I don't care
because
it is the most gentle breaking
the kind of breaking that feels exactly
like healing
I am falling
I am falling so hard
for you

"Jigsaw Heart"

Something inside of her was broken.
A kite without a string.
A bird without wings.
A heart without a beat.

Something inside of her fractured.
A wishbone.
The foundation of the wishing well.
Her hope.

There were days
when the pain was smooth, still water.
And others when it was a raging
sea, a hurricane of agony.

And she was drowning.
Endlessly drowning, and never dying.

But the waves,
tsunami level waves, ceased for a few seconds.

There were heartbeats when she could breathe
without sinking a little more.

Maybe she didn't need wings.
Maybe she just needed to be able to swim.

The broken pieces never fit together
again, never became wings,

but she put the shards back together.
The pieces fit better this time.
A puzzle rearranged into a different picture.

The kite wasn't flying.
There were no birds.

But there was floating,
and swimming,
and hope.

And a beating heart,
unbreakable.

Holly Wright

"even when we break"

this world is a dark place

sometimes it feels like all the lighthouses have burned out
and the black waves are gnashing higher
ready to consume us

but there are a trillion stars
pinpricks in the blackness

small lights
small hopes

that soon we'll be able to see again
hold them tight in your fist
don't let anyone take your hope from you
however small it is

it's okay to be weak
the wishbone was always my favorite part
it's okay to fall
haven't you ever wished on a star?

it's okay to break
even shatter

mosaics are beauty made of broken
so are we

"On Falling In Love"

It took me years to realize what falling
in love looked like

I thought it was roses
jewelry
giggly dates
and chocolate

Lots of chocolate

I watched the people around me
not just fall
but fall so hard their lives were meteors
engulfed in flames when they
crashed through the atmosphere

Totally life altering
Totally awe inspiring

Totally destructive

I didn't know then that love could be gentle
That love doesn't have to be loud

I know platonic love like the back of my hand
I know it because a boy I've never pictured
myself in a romantic comedy montage with
is the one that drove me to the hospital
after the weight of my rage finally cracked my spine
He's the scar on my left hand where
my disease was treated

Holly Wright

I know it because a boy who had a crush on me
and smacked my ass on a dare
is the same one that made sure I knew I was loved
while I cried
drunk and agonized
years later
over his best friend
He's the paper cut scar between my fingers
where my most loved book betrayed me

And I know the love of my mother
and my sister
and my brother
The smooth skin beneath the ring I never take off

But romantic love
that was foreign to me
An alien concept unfurling in front of me

I didn't know I knew what it was
the second I met you

It took me time to realize it
but love is a body of water
Shallow at first
and a little cold
shocking

The beginning of us was like that
a little cold
fragile
shocking

The Butcherknife and the Mockingbird

And then the ground dropped out
and we were floating in a new world
surprising and gentle
drenching our skin and dragging us down
We were treading water
learning secrets
telling jokes
making promises we couldn't comprehend

You made me remember what it feels like
to swim
To cut through the water like it's nothing
I was drowning for years
and you were my life preserver

That's what love became for me
An ocean
and you were the only thing keeping me afloat

It took time before I realized it
A thousand heartbeats before I realized
I'd rather sink next to you
in deafening blackness
than ever just tread water again with someone else

I think love became a comparison to water
because I looked in your eyes
once
and I drowned
I looked in your eyes the last time
and knew you were the place I always wanted
to return to

Holly Wright

I knew you like every scar on my hands
I want every scar
every freckle
every mark
to be you

I was never a meteor
not with you
I was never on fire
searing the world with my intensity
with my love

I was safe
I was quiet
I was alone with you

and somehow
the silence, the ripples
in our ocean
meant so much more
than the inferno
I had come to think
I needed

"The Bluebird"

There's a bluebird in my chest
and he sings, sometimes, and tries to escape

I hid him
for years
because I was 13
when I begged God
to give my heartbeat to a baby
that never took a breath

I was 13
when I found it takes more
courage
to slit your skin open
and see what amount
of pain
it takes to bleed
than it does to pitch
yourself from a 40-foot cliff

(I did that
once
I screamed
the entire way down)

I was 13 when I discovered
the kind of agony
that brings a person to their knees
And I don't mean in prayer

Holly Wright

I mean Mary anguished
I mean Daedalus gladly
following his son to the grave
I mean Atlas crumbling

Do you know how heavy
the weight of the grief must be
to reduce the man who carries the weight
of the world on his shoulders
to nothing?

I could feel the bluebird's wings
fluttering near my heart
and I had to keep him hidden
keep him safe

It took me three years
to find my way back to my feet
To find a steady place to stand
It took me three years to stop
talking to God like I thought he was there
and to finally stop tearing my flesh open
in the hopes that I could force the pain out

In two more years
I was a grown woman
I was still dreaming
of the fall
still looking at the sun
and going blind
I was eighteen
and convinced I'd seen all the joy

89

The Butcherknife and the Mockingbird

and suffering
I could ever imagine

The bluebird kept my heart safe

Some days there is ash in my lungs
Some days my entire world
is on fire
and I'm inhaling the ruins
choking on destruction
crashing to the waves
crashing to my knees while the weight of the world
shatters my spine
and my will to live

But there are nights
nights when my lungs are bursting
with cool
clear air
and I am not falling
I am soaring

And the bluebird in my chest
is singing
singing
singing

There is a bluebird in my chest
He sings, and wants to get out

And I'm letting him out

"The Vow"

I don't have much I can promise
I have less I can give

But this is what I have

My heart
bruised and battered and still in pieces

and a promise
that even when I want to walk away

(and I will want to
god I'll want to
I'll want to run
screaming
sometimes, like I'm fleeing a burning building)

I will hold on
I will stay

I will choose you

For the rest of my life
for the rest of yours
I will pick you,
when I loathe you
when I love him
when I want to move on

The Butcherknife and the Mockingbird

I will choose you
over
and over
and over

You have my heart,
my love

and my vow
that I will never do to your heart
what was done to mine

With me
your heart will always
be safe

Holly Wright

"The Mockingbird"

Mockingbirds sing only to please

I can't carry a tune,
but I'm singing anyway
because I finally can

(because I'm finally not screaming
instead)

and it's to please no one but myself

Can you hear my off-key song?
My tone deaf joy?

That's okay
This is my gift

This is for me

www.ingramcontent.com/pod-product-compliance
Lightning Source LLC
Chambersburg PA
CBHW031314130726
47988CB00007B/2828